D0717330

Jungle Animals

Written by Anita Ganeri
Illustrated by Michael Posen

p

This is a Parragon Book
This edition published in 2002

Parragon
Queen Street House
4 Queen Street
Bath BA1 1HE, UK

ISBN 0-75259-303-X

Printed in China

Produced by
Monkey Puzzle Media Ltd

Cover design: Design Principals

Contents

How many animals live in the rainforests?

ALTHOUGH RAINFORESTS COVER ONLY ABOUT A TENTH OF THE EARTH'S surface, they are home to at least half of the world's species of animals and plants – that's thousands of insects alone. About 1.5 million people also live in the rainforests.

What is being done to save them?
All over the world, conservation groups are working hard to save the rainforests. If the destruction is not stopped, the forests will disappear in 50 years time. We will then lose millions of animals, plants and precious resources like rainforest plants that could be used to make medicine.

Where do rainforests grow?
Rainforests grow along the Equator in the areas called the tropics, which are hot, sticky and steamy all year round. The biggest forests grow in South and Central America and South-east Asia. There are also smaller forests in China, Australia, India, Madagascar, Papua New Guinea and on some of the islands in the Caribbean. Many other countries can claim to have tiny scraps of rainforest.

Where is the biggest rainforest?
The world's biggest rainforest grows in South America, along the banks of the River Amazon. It is bigger than all the other rainforests put together. At 6,437 km (3,862 miles), the River Amazon is the world's second longest river, next to Egypt's River Nile.

Where do most rainforest animals live?
Most rainforest animals, from large, sleepy sloths to tiny insects, live in the thick layer of trees that makes up the canopy. This is the layer that gets most sun and rain. Here the trees produce plenty of fruit, seeds, leaves and flowers – a feast for the animals.

The jaguars like to live close to water where they can fish for food.

Jaguar

Why are they called rainforests?

Because of where they grow, rainforests are hot and wet all year round. There are no real seasons – just hot and wet, and even hotter and wetter. On the wettest days, up to 250 mm (10 in) of rain can fall, and there are thunderstorms in the afternoons.

Are rainforests the same as jungles?

You often hear rainforests called jungles, and the two words mean much the same thing. The word jungle comes from an old Indian word for a thick tangle of plants and trees. Jungle is a more poetic word, rainforest a more scientific word.

Why are rainforests being cut down?

Rainforests were once twice the size they are today, and they are disappearing fast. To clear land for farming and cattle ranching, the forests are being cut down and burned at the rate of 60 soccer pitches worth every single minute.

The rainforest canopy

Little sunlight reaches the forest floor, which is dark, gloomy and thick with rotting leaves.

How do rainforests grow?

Rainforests grow in layers, depending on the height of the trees. At the very top is the emergent layer where the tallest trees poke out above the rest. Beneath is a thick layer of treetops called the canopy, growing like a leafy, green umbrella over the rainforest. Below that is the understorey, made up of smaller trees and saplings.

Are there more animals to be discovered?

YES, THERE ARE! SCIENTISTS BELIEVE THAT THERE MAY BE MANY MORE ANIMALS, especially insects, that they have never seen or identified. Every so often, they discover a new one. Part of the problem is that many rainforest animals are nocturnal – they only come out at night. Others rarely venture down from their treetop homes.

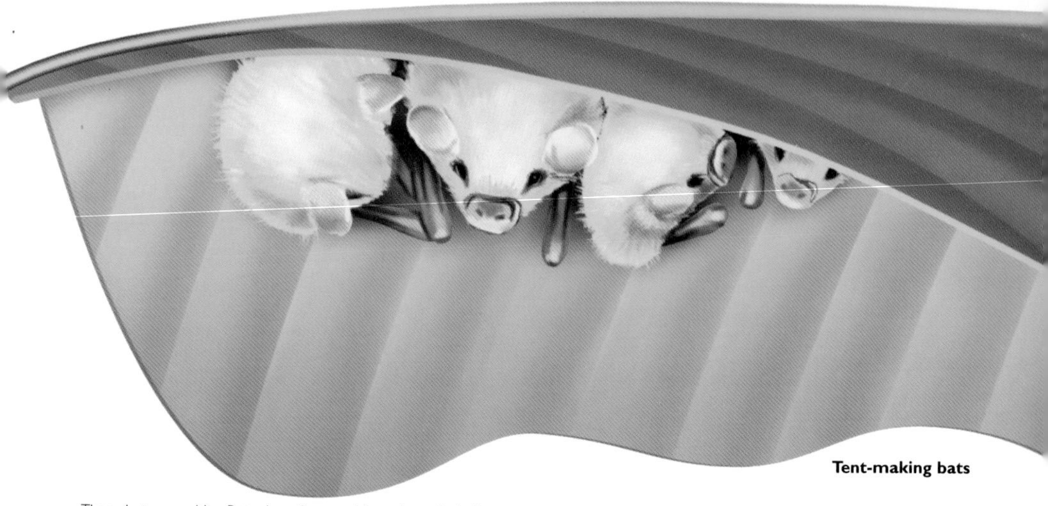

Tent-making bats

These bats are white. But when the sun shines through their green tent walls, the bats take on a greenish tinge which hides them from enemies.

Which bats make tents?

ONE TYPE OF SOUTH AMERICAN BAT, THE TENT-MAKING BAT (*Ectophylla alba*), makes a tent-like shelter from a large leaf, with the leaf still attached to its tree. The bats chew away along either side of the leaf's mid-rib so that the leaf hangs down on either side – just like a tent! Then they spend the day roosting underneath, clinging on to the mid-rib with their claws.

Which insects live in a tower?
Termites are tiny creatures, no bigger than grains of rice. They live in the rainforests of Africa, Asia and South America, in huge groups many millions strong. Some termites build tower-like nests on the forest floor, made of chewed-up wood, glued together with spit. Others build their nests in trees.

Who lives in a tree ant's nest?
Tree ants, of course! But when the tree ants move out, birds called trogons move in. These brightly coloured rainforest birds from Africa, Asia, Central and South America do not build their own nests. Instead, they dig holes in abandoned tree ants' nests and lay their eggs inside.

Which birds hang their nests from trees?
In the rainforests of South America, oropendola birds build nests hanging from tree branches. One tree may be home to hundreds of birds. The nests look a bit like saggy string bags, over 1 m (3 feet) long. The birds like to share their tree with bees, because the bees keep harmful flies away from their chicks.

Which kangaroo lives in trees?
Most kangaroos are adapted for hopping about on the ground. But not all! In Papua New Guinea, several types live up in the forest canopy. To help them climb, they have strong front arms for gripping the trees and wide feet with non-slip soles.

Who lives in a treehouse and eats monkeys?
Giant eagles, such as the monkey-eating eagle of the Philippines and the South American harpy eagle, live high up in the tops of the emergent trees. They swoop through the canopy on the look-out for monkeys to eat. The eagles build huge twig platforms in the treetops where they lay their eggs. They use the same nest year after year.

Where do gorillas sleep?

AT NIGHT, A GORILLA WILL FIND A SAFE PLACE TO SLEEP ON THE ground or in the trees. Then it builds itself a cosy bed from branches and leaves. This takes about five minutes. Then the gorilla snuggles down for a rest, pressing the bed into shape with its body. Gorillas live in tiny patches of rainforest in Africa.

Orangutans are endangered because their forest homes are being chopped down.

Orangutan

What do orangutans use as umbrellas?

It rains almost every day in the rainforest. Some animals don't mind the rain, but orangutans try to avoid a soaking. If they are caught in a shower, they pick a large leaf for an umbrella and shelter beneath it until the rain stops. Orangutans live in the rainforests of Borneo and Sumatra in South-east Asia.

What is a bushmaster?

A BUSHMASTER IS A HUGE AND DEADLY POISONOUS VIPER from Central and South America. It lies curled up on the forest floor, waiting for a juicy rat or small animal to pass by. The snake's brown markings keep it perfectly hidden among the dead leaves on the ground. Its prey does not see it until it is too late. Humans should watch out too. Its poison could kill you within a few hours!

Which creepy-crawly lives under a trapdoor?
Trapdoor spiders dig a burrow in the forest floor and cover it with an earth trapdoor. The spider lurks in its burrow, the door half-open, until something tasty to eat walks by. Then it pounces, drags the prey underground and slams the trapdoor shut.

Which bird uses its head like a battering ram?
Cassowaries are huge birds that live in the rainforests of Australia and Papua New Guinea. They crash through the undergrowth, using the big, bony growths on their heads like battering rams to push aside plants and rummage for food.

What is slimy and mouldy?
Slime moulds are very strange life-forms that live on the rainforest floor in South America. They slither over fallen tree trunks, like a slimy animal, in search of food. But they scatter spores, like plants, which grow into new slime moulds. Weird! They're actually half fungus and half bacteria.

Trapdoor spider

Trapdoor spiders come from Central America.

What's flat and slithers along the forest floor?
During a downpour, long, colourful flatworms ooze along the forest floor in rainforests all over the world. They can measure up to 15 cm (6 in) long. Flatworms are fierce hunters, able to gobble up snails more than twice their size. Their striking orange, black and yellow colours warn enemies to stay well away.

Tapirs are very good swimmers. They are threatened with extinction.

Malayan tapir

Why are tapirs black and white?
You might think that a Malayan tapir's black and white stripes would make it stick out like a sore thumb! But the opposite is true. The stripy pattern actually helps the tapir to hide among the patches of light and shade on the rainforest floor. Baby tapirs are born with a pattern of spots and stripes for even better camouflage. They lose these markings when they are eight months old.

How did the elephant shrew get its name?
From its long, trunk-like nose! These little creatures are about the size of rats with long, twitchy noses, like miniature elephants' trunks. They use their trunks to gather food on the forest floor in Africa and to sniff out termites and other insects.

Which frog looks like a leaf?

IS IT A LEAF? IS IT A FROG? WITH THE HORNED FROG, IT'S HARD TO tell. Its brown markings, combined with the small spiky horns on its head, which give it its name, make the perfect disguise. Hiding on the forest floor in the Amazon rainforest, it looks just like a wrinkled dead leaf.

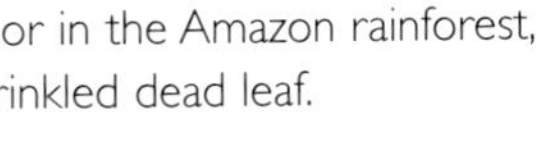

Why do tenrecs spit?

A TENREC IS A PRICKLY, HEDGEHOG-LIKE ANIMAL FROM MADAGASCAR. It sets out its territory by spitting on the spot it wants to mark, then rubbing its own strong body smell on to the wet spot. Other tenrecs recognise the smell and stay away.

Which animal burps a lot?
Male orangutans of South-east Asia burp loudly to warn other males to keep out of their territory. They fill the saggy pouches of skin around their throats with air, then let out a long call that starts off as a loud roar and ends with bubbling burps and groans.

Which is the quietest rainforest animal?
The tapirs of South America and Asia are very shy, secretive animals. They make hardly any noise at all for fear of being heard by hungry enemies such as jaguars and other big cats. Often the only sign that a tapir has been about is a line of its three-toed tracks.

Why does the mouse deer stamp its feet?
Mouse deer live in Asia. They are about the size of hares, with short, thin legs. They stamp their tiny feet to signal to each other. Mouse deer are extremely nervous. When they are startled, they freeze, then run away in a zig-zag through the forest.

Which animals use their tails like flags?
When ring-tailed lemurs go for a walk through the forests of Madagascar to patrol their territory, each lemur keeps its stripy tail raised high in the air. This is a signal to the other lemurs, like someone waving a flag. It shows them where each lemur is and helps to keep the group together. The lemurs mark the trees in their territory with a smelly scent to warn other ring-tails to keep out.

Why do tarsiers have such big eyes?
Tarsiers are tiny, monkey-like animals from South-east Asia. They come out to feed at night. They use their enormous eyes and sensitive ears to help them locate their prey of insects, lizards and birds in the dark. Then they leap through the branches, grab their prey in both hands and gobble it down head first.

Mouse deer have two teeth that stick out from their top jaw.

Mouse deer

Black howler monkey

The howler monkey has a special voice box that allows it to howl loudly.

Which bird sounds like a bell?
To attract a mate, the male bellbird of Central and South America opens its mouth wide and makes a call that sounds like a large, clanging bell. The bellbird has the loudest voice of any bird, so loud it can be heard a kilometre or more away.

Which monkey turns red with rage?
Many monkeys have brightly coloured skin or hair to signal to others. The odd-looking uakari lives in the rainforests of South America. Its face goes red if it is angry or excited. Uakaris also go bright red in the sun.

Which rainforest animal shouts loudest?

OF ALL THE ANIMALS IN THE RAINFOREST, THE HOWLER monkey has the loudest voice. It lives high up in the forests of South America. Every morning and evening, groups of howler monkeys wail and roar in an ear-splitting chorus. They do this to defend their own special patch of forest and their own particular food trees. You can't miss their call. Their voices are so loud that they can be heard some 8 km (5 miles) away.

Which animal uses semaphore?
It can be difficult to be heard in the noisy rainforests of South America. So many animals turn to colour to attract attention. Frogs usually communicate by croaking, but if it's too noisy, they wave their brightly coloured legs at each other in a type of froggy semaphore.

Which animals squeeze their prey to death?

Snakes called boas kill their prey by squeezing. The grey tree boa, for example, lives in the understorey of the African rainforest and preys on small mammals and birds. It head butts its prey to stun it, wraps its coils around it until it suffocates, then swallows it whole.

Why do macaws eat soil?

MACAWS USUALLY EAT FRUIT AND SEEDS FROM RAINFOREST TREES where they live in South America. But occasionally they gather along the river bank to peck away at the earth. This provides them with vital minerals lacking in their normal diet.

Which vines eat frogs?

Vine snakes hang down head-first from the trees in rainforests all over the world, looking just like harmless vines or creepers. But when an unsuspecting frog or lizard goes by, the vine darts out, catches it and gobbles it up!

Which spiders spin the biggest webs?

The biggest, strongest spider webs are built by golden orb-weaver spiders of Papua New Guinea. Their gigantic wheel-shaped webs can measure 1.5 m (5 feet) across. The "guy-ropes" that support the webs are even longer, measuring an astonishing 6 m (19 feet) in length.

Lemurs are closely related to monkeys and live in trees.

Aye-aye

Which is the fiercest rainforest hunter?

The jaguar is king of the South American rainforest. A fierce hunter, it patrols the forest on the look-out for tapirs, deer and wild pigs to eat. Sometimes it drops down on its prey from a tree. It is also a fast swimmer, chasing after fish and even alligators.

Which animal uses its fingers like forks?

The aye-aye is a very rare lemur from Madagascar. It uses its long, spindly middle fingers like forks to dig out juicy grubs from under tree bark. To locate the grubs, it knocks on the bark and listens for signs of movement.

What makes the orchid bee drunk?

The orchid bees of South America carry pollen from one gongora orchid to another to fertilise the plants. The orchid has a cunning way of enticing the bee into its flower. It produces a chemical that makes the bee drunk. It then tumbles into the flower and drops its load of pollen.

What can strip the meat off a cow in minutes?

Piranhas are small, snappy fish with a terrible reputation. The deadliest of all freshwater fish, they live in the rivers of South America. They usually prey on other fish, but may attack larger animals that fall into the water or come there to drink, such as tapirs, horses and cows. Not all piranhas eat meat. Some are harmless vegetarians, living on a diet of fruit!

Piranhas

With their razor-sharp teeth, a shoal of hungry piranhas can strip an animal to the bone in a matter of minutes.

Vampire bat

Bats' wings have long finger and arm bones that suport it as it flies.

Which rainforest bats drink blood?

FORGET HORROR FILMS AND COUNT DRACULA! REAL VAMPIRES LIVE IN the rainforests of Central and South America. Vampire bats live on a diet of blood, from horses, cows, goats and, occasionally, humans. They hunt at night, attacking animals as they sleep. A bat lands on its prey and takes a bite with its sharp, pointed teeth. Then it laps up the blood with its tongue. Its saliva contains a substance that stops blood clotting so it keeps flowing freely from the wound.

How does the fishing bat catch its supper?

The fishing bat of South America hunts for its food using sound. It make a series of high clicking noises that hit ripples in the water. By listening out for the echoes, the bat can tell not only where the ripples are but also locate the fish that made them.

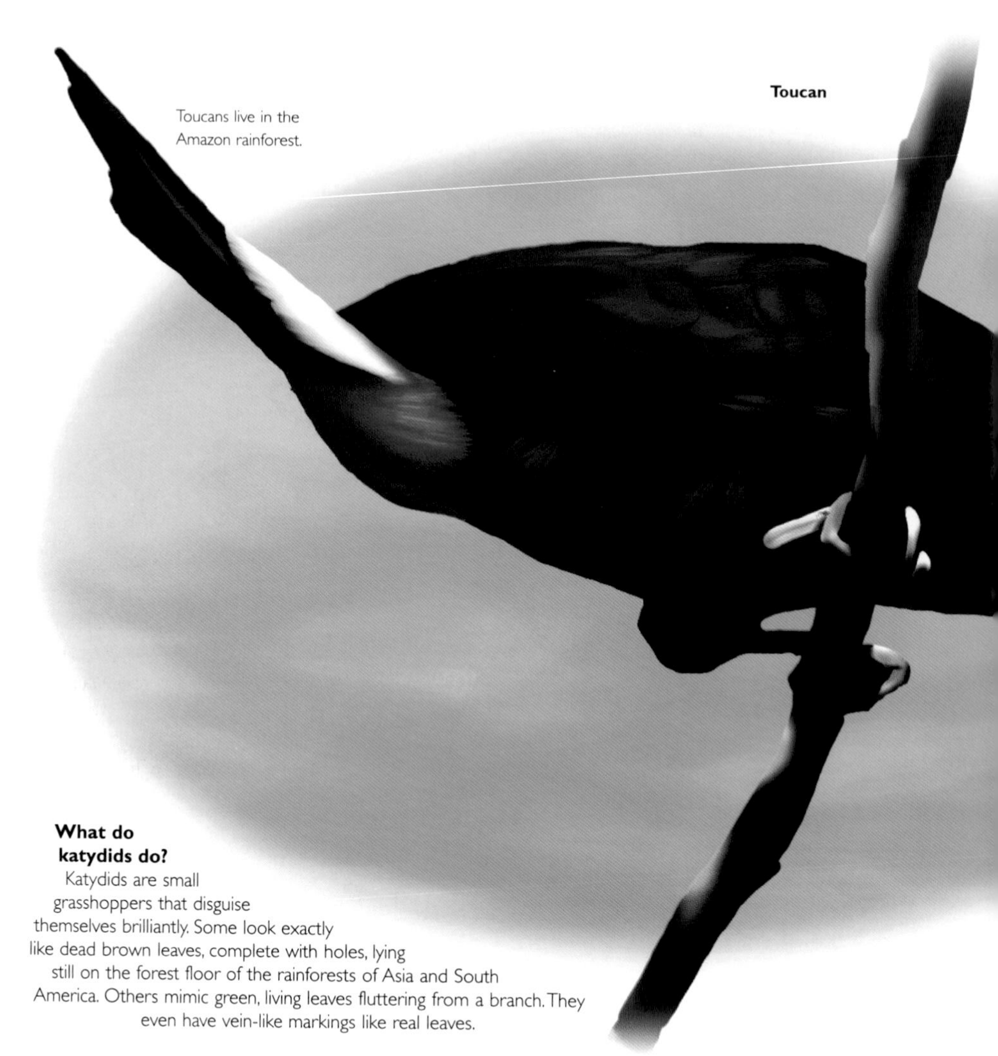
Toucan

Toucans live in the Amazon rainforest.

What do katydids do?

Katydids are small grasshoppers that disguise themselves brilliantly. Some look exactly like dead brown leaves, complete with holes, lying still on the forest floor of the rainforests of Asia and South America. Others mimic green, living leaves fluttering from a branch. They even have vein-like markings like real leaves.

Why do sloths have green fur?

SLOTHS ARE SO SLOW-MOVING THAT TINY GREEN PLANTS CALLED algae grow on their coats. This helps to camouflage the sloth among the trees of the rainforests of Central and South America. The algae provides food for the moth caterpillars that also live happily on the sloth's fur.

Which rainforest insect looks like a flower?

In the rainforest, things aren't always what they seem. Many animals are cleverly disguised as twigs, leaves, bark and even flowers. This hides them from hungry enemies and allows them to sneak up on prey unawares. The exquisite orchid mantis of Malaysia looks just like a beautiful flower, right down to its delicate petals. The mantis lurks on a twig, ready to shoot out its arms and grab interested insects such as flies and butterflies.

Why do tigers have stripes?

A TIGER'S STRIPES HELP TO HIDE IT AMONG THE UNDERGROWTH as it stalks or lies in wait for its prey. Its black and gold stripes break up the outline of its body, making it more difficult to see. Today, tigers are very rare. A very few still live in the rainforests of Asia.

Which butterflies keep vanishing?
As a *Morpho* butterfly flies through the rainforest trees of South America, it seems to vanish, then reappear. This is because its wings are brilliant electric-blue on top and brown underneath. Each beat of its wings produces a flash, like a strobe light.

Which animal can change colour?
Chameleons are masters of disguise. Their skin is usually green or brown but they can change colour to blend in with their background or show that they are angry or frightened. They do this by enlarging or shrinking special colour cells in their skin. Chameleons live in the rainforests of Asia and Africa.

Why do toucans have such colourful beaks?
Toucans are famous for their striking beaks, which can grow longer than their bodies. They use their beaks for reaching over and plucking fruit from branches. The bright colours may help the toucans to recognise each other and to scare off other birds.

What disguises itself as a bird dropping?
The crab spider! To take their insect prey by surprise, some crab spiders are disguised as bird droppings sitting on a leaf. Even at close range, it's difficult to tell the difference. Crab spiders live in rainforests all over the world. They get their name from the way they scuttle about like tiny crabs.

What makes a leaf-tailed gecko invisible?
The leaf-tailed gecko of Madagascar spends the day head-down on a tree trunk. You might think that this would make it an easy target for enemies – but you'd be wrong! The gecko is superbly camouflaged. Its dappled green-brown skin matches the colour of the bark perfectly. Its large, flat tail and ragged frill of skin make it look just like a woody bump.

Geckos often stick out their big, red tongues to scare attackers away!

Gecko

Pangolin

Which animal looks like a pine cone?

A pangolin is like a type of anteater covered in hard, sharp scales that overlap like the tiles on a roof. This provides the pangolin with a tough, armour-plated coat. When danger threatens, the pangolin curls up into a tight ball, like a large pine cone, to protect its soft belly. They eat ants and termites, which they lap up with their long, thin tongues.

Pangolins live in Asia and Africa.

Which butterfly has two heads?

IT'S DIFFICULT TO TELL ONE END OF A HAIRSTREAK BUTTERFLY FROM the other. This butterfly from South America has a dummy head on its back wings, complete with false antennae. This tricks birds into attacking the wrong end of the butterfly and leaving its real head alone.

What makes a cockroach hiss?

In the rainforests of Madagascar, big brown cockroaches come out at night to forage for fungi and fallen leaves, especially after rainfall. Some grow up to 10 cm (4 in) long! To scare away attackers and warn off rivals, the cockroaches make a loud hissing sound, by pushing air out through two holes on their sides. Males also hiss more gently to attract a female cockroach for mating.

Which spiders throw sticks?

FROM THEIR RESTING PLACE IN THE TREETOPS, THE SPIDER MONKEYS OF Central and South America sometimes throw twigs and small branches at intruders to scare them away from their home territory. So if things start landing on your head on a rainforest walk, you know who to blame!

How sharp are a wild boar's tusks?
Very sharp indeed! Wild boars live in some parts of Asia. They use their tusks as weapons for fighting off rivals for a mate and for defending themselves against enemies. The tusks are actually overgrown canine teeth, growing upwards from the boar's lower jaws.

Which caterpillar acts like a snake?
Caterpillars make tasty meals for rainforest birds. To scare off hungry predators, the hawkmoth caterpillar waves its body to look like a miniature snake. It also flashes the big false eyes on its underside to make it look more threatening. Hawkmoths live in rainforests all over the world.

Which animal blows up like a balloon?
The huge rococo toad from South America protects itself from hungry enemies by oozing out poison from behind its head. It also gulps in air to blow itself up to the size of a small balloon. This makes it almost impossible to swallow.

Why do some moths have four eyes?
When it is resting on the forest floor in South America, the wild silk moth is perfectly camouflaged to look like a leaf. But if a lizard or bird tries to have a closer look, the moth flashes the huge, staring eyespots on its back wings to frighten it away.

Which fish could give you a nasty shock?
Electric eels live in slow, sluggish streams in the Amazon rainforest. They use electricity, made in their muscles, to stun their prey and make it easier to swallow, and to warn off would-be attackers. They can also give humans a nasty shock.

Electric eel

The electric eel has special organs in its body that produce electricity.

Fer-de-lance snake

There are 2700 types of snake, but only 400 are poisonous.

Which snake was once used as a weapon?

The fer-de-lance is a deadly poisonous snake that grows up to 2.5 m (8 feet) long. It is said that local people in South America used to slip these snakes into tubes and use them as lethal weapons to fire at their enemies.

How do arrow-poison frogs get their name?

THE BRIGHTLY COLOURED SKIN OF A SOUTH AMERICAN arrow-poison frog is a signal to would-be attackers. It warns them that the frog is very nasty indeed to eat. The frog's slimy skin is deadly poisonous. Forest people extract the poison and use it to tip their hunting arrows. And this is how arrow-poison frogs get their name.

Which animal has a sting in its tail?

If you're out and about in rainforests all over the world, particularly at night, watch out for scorpions. They have a sting in their tails, loaded with deadly poison. A scorpion uses its tail mainly in self-defence, and holds it curled above its body, ready to strike.

What would happen if you trod on a stingray?

You'd get a painful shock! Stingrays are usually quite harmless unless you go and step on one. Sharp poisonous spines grow near the end of their long thin tails. If disturbed, a stingray whips its tail round and stabs the spine into its attacker. Stingrays live in the Amazon River in South America.

Arrow-poison frog

Which animal shoots boiling poison at its enemies?
Bombardier beetles have a very unusual and unpleasant way of warning off enemies. When provoked, the beetle swivels the tip of its abdomen round and shoots a spray of boiling hot, poisonous chemicals at its attacker. The spray is made inside the beetle's body, from two otherwise quite harmless chemicals. They react together with an explosive sound loud enough for you to hear. There's no escape – the beetle has a very accurate aim!

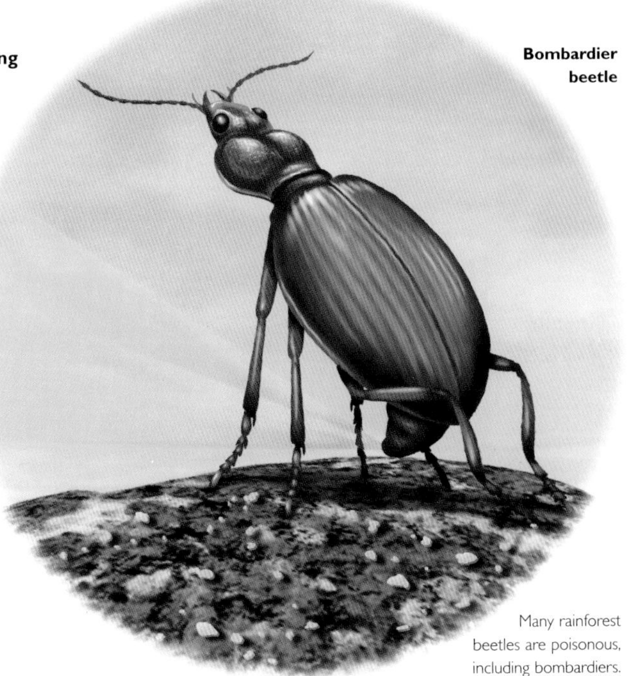
Bombardier beetle

Many rainforest beetles are poisonous, including bombardiers.

How do people get poison from arrow-poison frogs?
To extract poison from arrow-poison frogs, South American hunters roast the frogs over a fire so that the poison oozes out. The poison is so deadly that the hunters have to wrap their hands in leaves for protection.

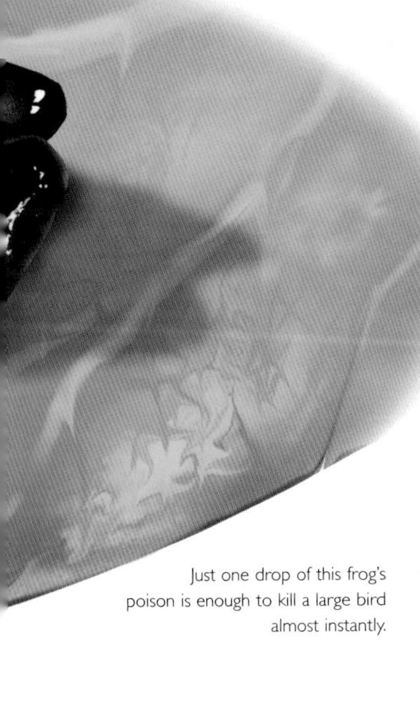
Just one drop of this frog's poison is enough to kill a large bird almost instantly.

Do centipedes have a poisonous bite?
Centipedes are fierce hunters and their first pair of legs is modified into fangs. These are used to inject poison into prey. Most centipedes are small and harmless to people. But large centipedes can pack an agonisingly painful bite. Centipedes live in rainforests all over the world.

Which snake pretends to be poisonous?
For some rainforest animals, pretending to be poisonous is the next best thing to being poisonous. In South America, harmless false coral snakes mimic the bright colours of extremely poisonous true coral snakes to trick their enemies into leaving them alone.

Are any birds poisonous?

UNTIL RECENTLY, SCIENTISTS DID NOT THINK SO. THEN, IN 1992, IT WAS found that the feathers and skin of the pitohui bird of Papua New Guinea contained a poison strong enough to kill mice and frogs. In people, it can cause numbness, burning and sneezing.

Spider monkeys live in Central and South America.

How do snakes climb trees?
Many rainforest snakes are excellent climbers. Their long, muscular bodies are good for slithering along the branches, and they have rough scales on their bellies to help them grip. Then they loop their coils over a branch and lie in wait for prey.

How do gibbons swing so fast?
Gibbons have arms that are longer than their bodies. This helps them to swing very fast through the trees. With its huge armspan, a gibbon can swing 10 or so metres (32 feet) from one branch to another in one go, gripping the branches with its long fingers. Gibbons live in the rainforests of South-east Asia.

How many legs does a spider monkey have?

THE ANSWER IS FOUR, LIKE ANY OTHER MONKEY! BUT SPIDER MONKEYS also use their long tails as an extra arm or leg for gripping on to branches. In fact, their tails are so strong that the monkeys can swing by their tails alone.

Are there dragons in the rainforest?
Yes, there are – flying dragons! These are a type of lizard. They have flaps of skin stretched between their front and back legs, on either side of their bodies. They use these like wings, to glide through the air from tree to tree in some of the Asian rainforests.

Can snakes fly?

SNAKES CAN'T REALLY FLY BECAUSE THEY DON'T HAVE WINGS. BUT some have a go. The paradise flying snake lives high up in the rainforest trees in Borneo. To set off in search of lizards to eat, it launches itself from a branch and flattens its body so that it can glide through the trees. These snakes are also excellent climbers, with sharp ridges on their bellies for grip. If they land in a tree with plenty of lizards to eat, they may not move off it for months on end.

What bird is like a helicopter?

Hummingbirds feed on nectar found deep inside rainforest flowers in South America. To reach its food, a hummingbird hovers in front of a flower like a tiny helicopter. It has to beat its wings up to 20 times a second, so quickly that they make a humming sound. Then the bird probes into the flower with its long, thin bill and laps up the nectar with its tube-like tongue. A hummingbird can also fly forwards and backwards, and up and down.

Which animals bounce across the ground?

Sifakas are lemurs from Madagascar. They can't run on all fours because their legs are much longer than their arms. Instead they bounce along the ground, hopping from one foot to the other, holding their arms up in the air.

Why do frogs have suckers on their feet?

Many rainforest frogs live high up in the trees to avoid hungry predators on the ground. They have to be good at climbing. To help them, they have pads of sticky hairs, like suckers, on their fingers and toes, and loose, sticky skin on their bellies.

Which creature performs a miracle?

The basilisk lizard of South America has an amazing ability. It walks on water! It literally runs across the surface of a pond or pool without sinking. It is thought that its sheer speed keeps it afloat, while its long tail helps it to balance.

Basilisk lizard

The basilisk lizard uses its water-walking skills to escape from enemies.

Why do glow-worms glow?

AT NIGHT, SOME RAINFOREST TREES ARE FILLED WITH TINY FLASHING lights. These are made by glow-worms or fireflies. They produce their yellow-green lights through chemical reactions inside their bodies. Glow-worms flash their lights in the dark to attract a mate. Each species has its own pattern of flashes, which other members of its species can recognise. Despite the name, glow-worms are actually a type of beetle.

Which baby bird has claws on its wings?

Hoatzins live in South America. They build their nests in trees that overhang rainforest rivers and streams. If danger threatens, hoatzin chicks simply dive headfirst into the river. When it is safe, the chicks climb slowly back up, using tiny claws on their wings to help them grip.

Hoatzin adult and chick

This hoatzin chick makes a dive for safety as its parent looks on.

Which bird imprisons itself in a tree?
In Africa, a female hornbill lays her eggs in a hole in a tree. Then, helped by her mate, she seals herself in, covering the entrance with droppings and mud. Only a tiny slit is left, through which the male delivers food. This keeps the nest safe from snakes until the chicks are old enough to leave the nest and learn how to fly.

Which tadpoles learn to swim in a plant?
Bromeliads are rainforest plants related to pineapples. They grow high up on tree branches in South America. Rainwater collects in tiny pools formed by their overlapping leaves. These pools are used as nurseries for arrow-poison frog tadpoles.

What wasp lays its eggs in the body of a live insect?
In many rainforests, female ichneumon wasps lay their eggs in the body of another insect while it is still alive. When the eggs hatch, the wasp grubs feed on the insect. They leave its vital parts until last, to keep it alive and fresh for longer. Scary!

Which minibeast carries its babies on its back?
A female scorpion carries her babies on her back to keep them safe from enemies. The babies cling on with their sharp pincers. If one falls off, their mother stops and waits for it to climb back on again. After a few days, they are ready to fend for themselves. Scorpions are found in rainforests all over the world.

Blue bird of paradise

Birds of paradise live in Australia and Papua New Guinea.

Which bird hangs upside down to show off?
The dazzling feathers of male birds of paradise give the birds their names. People thought that these birds were so stunning they could only come from paradise. The males use their feathers to attract a mate. The Count Raggi's bird of paradise, puts on a special courtship display. He hangs upside down from a branch to show off his magnificent orange feathers. After mating, he loses his feathers and has to grow them again the following year.

Which insect sings to its mate?

THE CICADA IS THE LOUDEST INSECT IN THE RAINFOREST. TO ATTRACT A mate, the male cicada clicks small plates of skin in its sides at a rate of more than 1,000 times a second. Meanwhile, it listens for a female to reply with a flick of her wings. Cicadas live in rainforests all over the world.

Which caterpillars live in a tent?
The tent-caterpillar moth of South America gets its name from the way its caterpillars live. They build fine, silk nests. among the rainforest trees. The adult moths are superbly camouflaged to blend in with the lichens growing on a tree trunk.

The bright yellow body of Queen Alexandra's birdwing shows that it is poisonous.

Queen Alexandra's birdwing

Which butterfly is as big as a bird?

THE QUEEN ALEXANDRA'S BIRDWING IS THE BIGGEST BUTTERFLY IN THE rainforest and in the world. It lives in Papua New Guinea, flitting among the tops of the rainforest trees. Female butterflies may have a wingspan of over 28 cm (11 in) – twice the width of your outstretched hand! Males are much smaller. Sadly, these beautiful creatures are now very rare because of overtrapping by collectors and the destruction of their forest home.

Are ants good at needlework?

Some are! Tailor ants make their nests from living leaves, still attached to the tree. Instead of needles and thread, they use a type of silk made in the mouths of their own grubs. The grubs are passed to and fro between the leaves to sew them together. These smart creatures live in the rainforests of Asia.

Why are grasshoppers flashy?

At rest, many rainforest grasshoppers are well camouflaged among the green leaves. But if they are disturbed, they fly away, flashing brightly coloured back wings. Then they land again, and seem to disappear to confuse their attacker.

What creature drinks several times its own weight in blood?
Leeches live in rainforests all over the world. They gorge themselves on blood, from animals and humans! They have suckers at either end of their bodies for clinging on to their prey. After they have fastened themselves to their victim, they make a cut in its flesh with their strong, sharp teeth and start to feed. A leech can drink several times its own weight in blood in one meal.

Which stick is really an insect?
Stick insects live in rainforests all over the world. They are long and thin, and perfectly camouflaged to look exactly like twigs or sticks. Some even have growths on their bodies and legs that mimic clumps of moss or lichen. These amazing insects can reach over 33 cm (13 in) long.

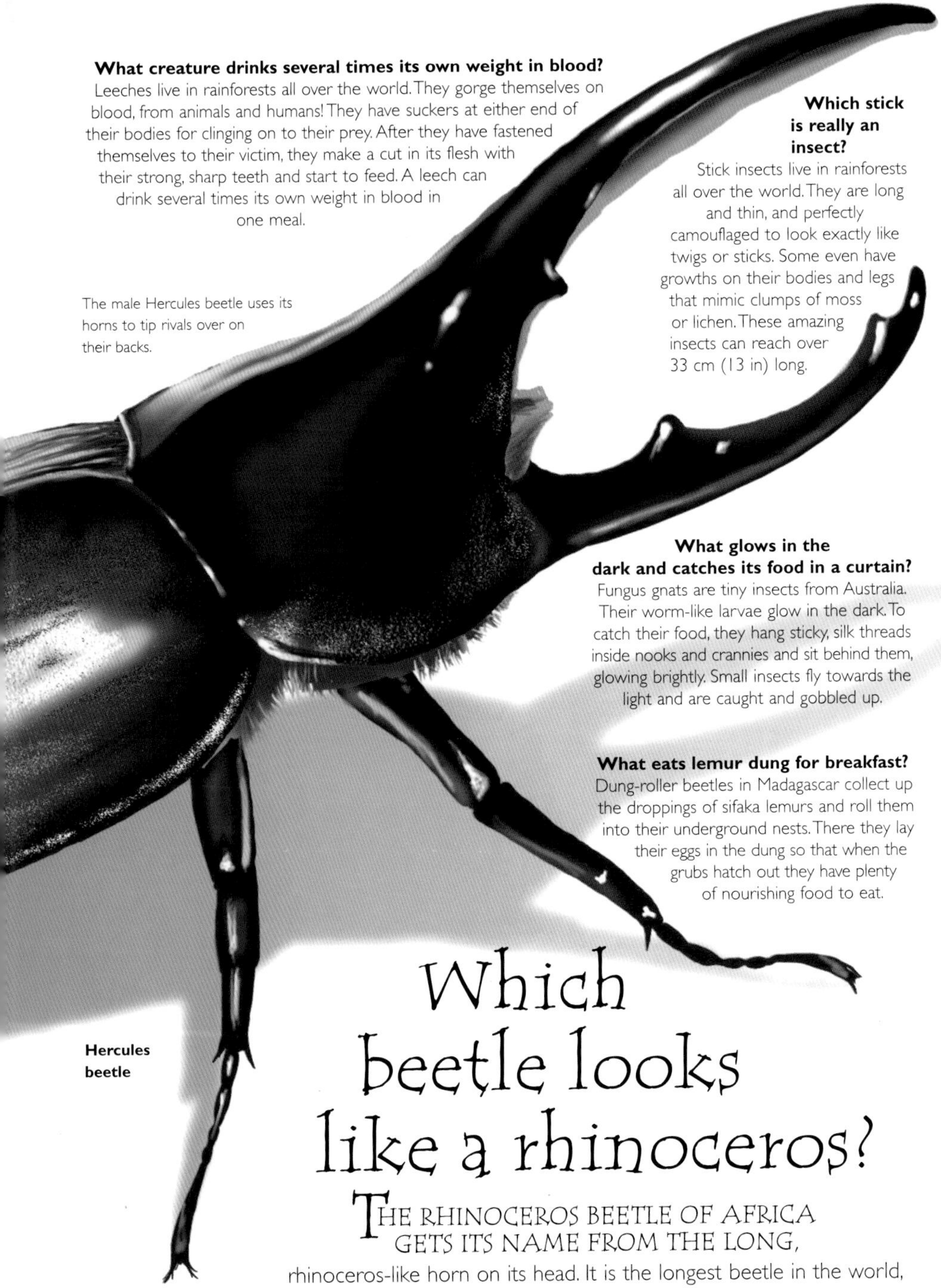

The male Hercules beetle uses its horns to tip rivals over on their backs.

What glows in the dark and catches its food in a curtain?
Fungus gnats are tiny insects from Australia. Their worm-like larvae glow in the dark. To catch their food, they hang sticky, silk threads inside nooks and crannies and sit behind them, glowing brightly. Small insects fly towards the light and are caught and gobbled up.

What eats lemur dung for breakfast?
Dung-roller beetles in Madagascar collect up the droppings of sifaka lemurs and roll them into their underground nests. There they lay their eggs in the dung so that when the grubs hatch out they have plenty of nourishing food to eat.

Hercules beetle

Which beetle looks like a rhinoceros?

THE RHINOCEROS BEETLE OF AFRICA GETS ITS NAME FROM THE LONG, rhinoceros-like horn on its head. It is the longest beetle in the world, measuring up to 19 cm (8 in), though more than half of this is horn.

Which rainforest bird helps people find honey?
The honeyguide is a small bird that lives in Africa and Asia. Like many rainforest birds, it feeds on insects, but its favourite food is beeswax. In Africa, honeyguides and local people help each other. The bird leads them to a bees' nest, flying and calling to show the way. Then men climb the tree and break the nest open. They take the honey and leave the beeswax for the bird to feast on.

When can a hyacinth fly?
The spectacular hyacinth macaw of South America is one of the rarest birds in the rainforest. It is also the world's largest parrot. Unfortunately, so much of its rainforest home has been destroyed and so many macaws have been captured for zoos and the pet trade that this beautiful bird is now facing extinction.

Which birds have the longest tails?
The male argus pheasant of Asia has the longest feathers of any flying birds. Its tail feathers often reach 1.7 m (6 feet) in length. Its long wing feathers are covered in "eyes". The male fans out these feathers to attract a mate.

Hyacinth macaw

It is thought that only 3,000 macaws are left in the wild.

How do sunbirds slurp up their food?
Like hummingbirds, sunbirds from Asia and Africa feed on nectar from rainforest flowers. They have long, thin beaks for reaching deep inside the flowers and long, tubular tongues for sucking up nectar as if through a straw.

What sleeps like a bunch of leaves?

HANGING PARROTS SLEEP HANGING UPSIDE DOWN FROM TREE branches. From a distance, the parrots look just like bunches of leaves, which makes them very tricky for enemies to spot. Hanging parrots live in the rainforests of Asia.

Which bird sniffs out its food?

Pittas are brightly coloured birds that live in South-East Asia. They forage for food on the rainforest floor. They mainly eat insects, worms and snails. They use their superb sense of smell to sniff out their prey from amongst the leaf litter and under the ground.

Cock-of-the-rocks

Cock-of-the-rocks live in Central and South America.

Which bird was worshipped as a god?

Quetzals are glittering green and crimson birds from Central America. In Aztec times, the quetzal was worshipped as the god of the air. Its trailing tail feathers, which can grow 60 cm (2 ft) long, were highly prized for making into costumes and head-dresses.

Why do cock-of-the-rocks like dancing?

Male cock-of-the-rocks are brilliant orange and black birds. To attract mates, the males clear a space on the forest floor and perform a type of dance. This includes spreading out their beautiful feathers to show off to females in the nearby trees.

How do antbirds avoid getting stung?

Antbirds follow armies of ants as they swarm through the South American rainforests. They don't eat the ants themselves but feed on other insects disturbed by the ants. A thick ruff of feathers around the birds' face stops it from getting painfully stung by the ants!

Giraffe-necked weevil

Which beetle looks like a giraffe?
The bizarre giraffe-necked weevil from Madagascar is one of the oddest-looking insects in the rainforest. Males have very long heads – about half the length of their bodies.

How does a turtle keep its nostrils dry?
The matamata turtle uses its long neck as a snorkel to hold its nostrils up out of the water. This means that it can breathe without moving and frightening away the fish on which it feeds. The turtle lives in muddy rivers in South America.

No one knows why this weevil has such a strange head.

Which flies' eyes pop out on stalks?
Diopsid flies live in many rainforests. They have eyes on the end of long stalks. No one is quite sure why. One idea is that the stalks look like wasps' antennae. Predators mistake the flies for wasps, which might sting if they get any closer.

Which bug has a lantern head?

THE LANTERN BUG FROM SOUTH AMERICA GOT its name because people once thought that its odd-shaped head glowed in the dark. In fact, its large head looks a bit like a miniature crocodile. It may be useful for scaring off enemies and stopping the bug from being eaten.

Which is the shyest rainforest animal?
The shyest animal in the rainforest is probably the okapi. These timid creatures are related to giraffes and look like a cross between a short-necked giraffe and a zebra. They live only in the rainforests of Zaire, Africa. Okapis are so secretive and solitary that, apart from local people, no one knew they even existed until 1901.

Okapi

Okapis are endangered because their forest homes are being destroyed and they are poached for their meat.

Which is the rarest rainforest animal?

So much of their forest home has been cleared to make space for coffee, rubber and banana plantations that there may be fewer than 250 golden lion tamarins left in the wild. The last remaining tamarins live in a few patches of rainforest along the Atlantic coast of Brazil. Efforts are being made to save the tamarins. If these fail, they could be extinct within just a few years.

Golden lion tamarin

Golden lion tamarins are illegally captured for the pet trade and zoos.

How many mountain gorillas are there?

THERE ARE THREE SEPARATE GROUPS OF MOUNTAIN GORILLAS, ALL IN THE rainforests of Central Africa. All three are endangered because of forest clearance and poaching for their meat. Scientists estimate that there may be fewer than 40,000 left in the wild.

What is white and pink and keeps its baby in its pocket?

A cuscus is a marsupial from Papua New Guinea. It has a pouch on its front where its young grow and develop. The cuscus has a thick white coat and a long tail with a bare pink tip. It uses its tail to help it climb through the trees.

What keeps its baby in a watertight pouch?

The yapok is a marsupial from Central and South America that is adapted for life in water. It has webbed back feet to help it swim after its prey of fish, frogs and crustaceans. Its pouch opens backwards so that it stays watertight when the yapok dives into the water.

Which spider is a big as a plate?
Including its eight hairy legs, a bird-eating spider, or tarantula, can grow as big as a plate. It's the biggest spider in the world and lives in South America. Bird-eating spiders hunt at night, on the rainforest floor. Despite their name, they very rarely catch birds.

Which rodent breaks records?
The world's biggest rodent is the capybara from South America. (Rodents are animals such as mice and rats.) It's about the size of a pig and lives around lakes, rivers and marshes. Its arch enemy is the jaguar, the fiercest hunter in the rainforest.

Are big animals the most dangerous?

NO, THEY'RE NOT! THE MOST DANGEROUS ANIMALS are small insects – mosquitoes. They spread malaria, a disease that kills millions of people a year. Symptoms include a raging fever. Mosquitoes can also pass on yellow fever and elephantiasis. They live in rainforests all over the world.

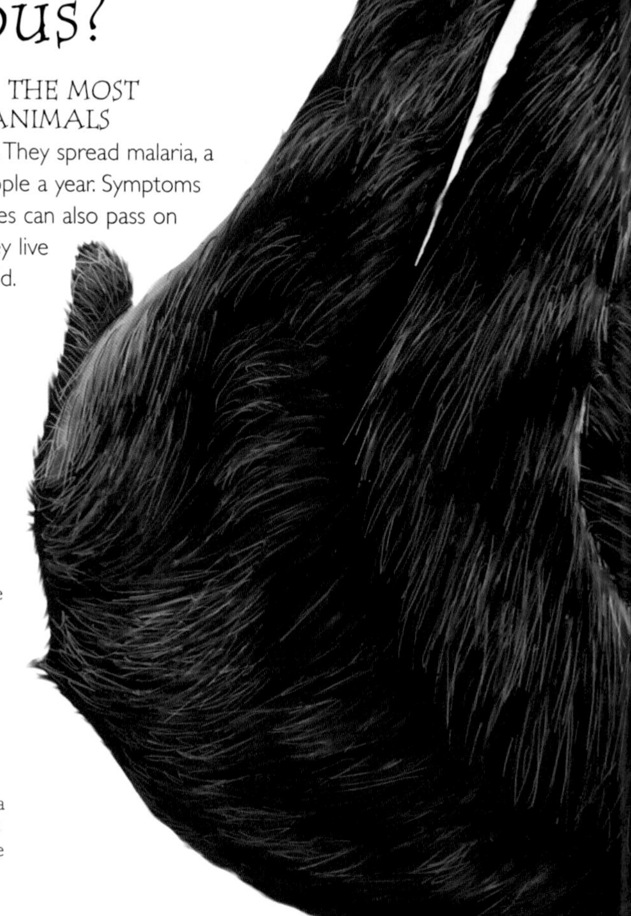
Three-toed sloth

The three-toed sloth even eats its food hanging upside down.

Which is the laziest rainforest animal?
The laziest animal in the rainforest has to be the three-toed sloth from South America. This idle animal spends about 18 hours a day hanging upside down from a tree branch, fast asleep. It spends the rest of the time looking for food. Unusually, its shaggy hair also grows upside down, from its belly towards its back. This is so that the rain runs off it more easily and the sleepy sloth does not get waterlogged!

Which bird builds the smallest nests?
The vervain hummingbird of South America builds a nest from plants and cobwebs that's only about the size of half a walnut shell. There it lays the smallest eggs of any bird, barely the size of peas. The bee hummingbird's nest is also tiny, about the size of a thimble.

Anaconda

Anacondas like to live in trees as well as in water.

Which is the biggest rainforest snake?

THE GIGANTIC ANACONDA OF SOUTH AMERICA IS THE WORLD'S BIGGEST snake. The heaviest on record was 8.45 m (27 feet) long, more than a metre (3 feet) round its middle and weighed almost a quarter of a tonne. Anacondas lurk in the water at the river's edge, with just their eyes and nostrils showing, waiting for their prey. They can kill prey as large as deer, goats and alligators, crushing them to death with their huge coils.

How big is the biggest moth in the rainforest?

The Hercules atlas moth from Australia and Papua New Guinea has a wingspan of up to 28 cm (11 in), and it may grow even bigger. The moth has long, feathery antennae for smelling, touching and telling how hard the wind is blowing.

Which animal has the biggest appetite?

You might think that the answer would be a jaguar or an alligator. In fact, it's the larva of the polyphemus moth, which lives in Central America. It eats a staggering 86,000 times its own birth weight in food in the first two days of its life!

Which bird is smaller than a butterfly?

The bee hummingbird of South America is the world's smallest bird. It measures 5.7 cm (just over 2 in) in length, nearly half of which is its bill and tail. This tiny creature is smaller than many of the butterflies and moths in its rainforest home.

Index

AB

CDE

FG

HIJK

LMN

OPQ

RS

TU

VWXYZ